2019 International Cultural Exchange Conference

- and -

2019 International Environment Protection Awareness Conference

Kevin Bryan and Derek Dong

TABLE OF CONTENTS

ACKNOWLEDGEMENTS

We would like to thank all of our guest speakers for attending our conferences and providing us with such insightful speeches. We also thank our hosts for keeping the conference running smoothly, as well as the technology department for making sure the powerpoint was working properly. Thank you to all the students who translated on stage, as well as those who transcribed and translated speeches for our proceedings.

Editors-in-Chief of Proceedings:
Kevin Bryan and Derek Dong

Conference Master of Ceremonies:
Will Wu, Kevin Bryan, Julie Broch, Jenny Wang

Conference Host:
Kevin Bryan, Julie Broch, Jenny Wang, Derek Dong, Yuhao Wang, Serena Mao, Christina Hua, Michael Chang, Erick Moises Xu Li, Yukiko Xian

Stage Translators:
Eileen Guo, Serena Mao, Jenny Wang, Zeru Peter Li, Will Wu

Proceedings Transcription:
Kevin Bryan, Derek Dong, Erick Moises Xu Li, Christina Hua, Michelle Hua

2019
International Cultural Exchange Conference

Location: Wuhan China; Date: June 23, 2019
Hosts of Conference: Kevin Bryan, Will Wu, Julie Broch

This has been the fifth annual International Cultural Exchange Conference. Our purpose for this conference is to have professionals and students exchange information and ideas about the differences between cultures ranging from the United States to China to Mexico, as well as providing insight into education abroad. We have translated, transcribed, compiled, and edited the speeches of all our speakers.

Proceeding editors: Kevin Bryan, Derek Dong

DR. JAY JONES

Professor Jones has a broad academic background, with concentrations in Botany, Microbiology, Chemistry, and Geology. His research and work experience includes Senior Research Geobotanist, conducting research on oil and gas exploration (ARCO), Naturalist/Interpreter (National Park Service), Remote Sensing Consultant (NASA/Lockheed). He is currently in the field conducting floral surveys, as well as in the laboratory working with complex analytical instrumentation. As Professor of Biology and Biochemistry, Jones has taught an exceptionally broad range of courses including versions of an interdisciplinary course entitled: Toward a Sustainable Planet. Many of these courses have field components in which faculty and students see the global impact of the human species in various countries around the world.

The Changing Face of American Higher Education

Today, I'm going to talk a little about education in the United States and the changes that are going on currently. How many of you are aspiring to study in the United States, can you raise your hands?

Some of you are anticipating going to the United States to be able to study. The question is, what school is going to be the best for you? Most people go to college in order to qualify for a job. We might want to become an engineer, or perhaps a doctor. However, one of the most valuable things about going to college is actually to broaden your perspectives, to learn what opportunities are available, and to find your passion. The other very important thing that higher education introduces to us is how to become an informed global citizen. We live in a world together. We are all connected. There is nothing that we do that doesn't affect other people in the world. The final reason that I think we go to college is to have a happy life, a quality life. In order to get that quality of life, you must find satisfaction not in money or your profession, but in the community. It is the relationship between you and the people around you that are the most satisfying and enriching things in life.

I will give you an example. 70% of students at the college level, at the undergraduate level, will change their major, abandon what they were going to be, to another path to finish their education. When I started college, I wanted to be a pharmacist, because I loved chemistry and biology. But when I got to college, I found many other opportunities, and a whole world that I didn't realize existed. I got involved in research and became closely associated with research scientists. I realized that I no longer wanted to be a pharmacist. I could no longer see myself behind a counter counting pills and reading prescriptions. That would be very boring for me.

I developed a passion for research and the environment. My current profession allows me to travel around the world, to get into indigenous areas to see wildlife, yet also be in a laboratory with high-tech instrumentation. It also helps to answer the big questions in life: who am I, and how am I related to the universe around me? My college environment opened doors to the world around me. Education also helped me to understand that values mean a lot. You develop the sense that what you do has an effect on the people you are with and people around the world. When you make informed decisions based on values, it is fulfilling and you feel good inside. When you are in college, a lot of education occurs not just in the classroom, not just with the professor, but with those around you.

Also, no matter where you go to study, make sure you include exposure to the arts, music, and nature. This is very near our campus, at San Antonio Peak. When I go there, I get a BIG picture, something that takes me away from the daily concerns of life. This is Walden Pond, those that have gone to Harvard, and are familiar with that, know the significance of Walden Pond. Every time I go to Boston, I walk around Walden Pond. When you go to college, you will be asked to take courses you don't THINK you need. I want to a dentist: why do I have to take geography? Why do I need to understand music? General education allows you to see the big picture. It also allows you to find your own passion and enriching aspects of life. Travel can be important in education. Seeing how other people live, seeing other cultural traditions, seeing more of the natural environment, and experiencing changes that are going on there are all important. I love coffee! But I realize that when I drink coffee, I am also supporting the deforestation of certain parts of the world. Putting spider monkeys and other animals out of a home. So now I am trying to concentrate on tea... But I still drink coffee.

So now the question is what university do I want to go to? Do I want to go to Harvard, do I go to Stanford, or do I go to some of these other institutions that have different unique qualities? Each university has its own strengths. Each student has their own strengths. Some students can do better in some schools. Other students can do better in others. How does one decide?

First, you must understand why you are going to college. What do you value? Does the prestige matter? Does geographical region matter? And from what university can you learn the most? I will tell you a little bit about the different options that exist in the United States.

Community colleges are the least expensive. They are the least competitive, but you can still get a very good education. If you are looking for exposure to an American university, this is not a bad option to let you see American culture and to see how you do in a U.S. academic environment. Then you could transfer, perhaps, to another university. Community college allows you to step into the American culture, become skilled in the language, and develop the ability to do well in the classroom.

Another type of school is a 4 year school, with a master's program, with no doctorate. This kind of school provides more comprehensive courses, more challenging courses, and more enrichment in each individual major. The final class is what we call the comprehensive doctoral-granting university. These are the universities that grant a doctorate degree. They are focused on research, so sometimes they focus less on the undergraduates themselves.

Let's talk about the comprehensive R1 institutions. These are the ones with the highest reputation. These are the ones where you will find high-level research being conducted. If you have found academic success and if your language skills are excellent, this is probably the place for you. These institutions allow you to be in touch with top-notch researchers as well as build relationships with other high achievers. R2 schools are also doctoral-granting but are not necessarily top-ranked schools. These schools are also a good option, but it depends on what field you are going into.

However, you should beware of the for-profit high education schools, schools like the University of Phoenix. They spend most of their money on marketing and very little on actual education. Unfortunately, the marketing works well very frequently with foreign students, and they get lured into these programs and end up paying a lot of money with very little to show for it. Although I must say, that even within the state schools and traditional schools, we now are experiencing a trend that is concentrating more on enrollments and less on the quality of education. We now have far more administrators than we have tenured faculty. Research grant overhead provides the incentive to focus on research rather than education.

The education that I was able to have was the most valuable thing in my life. Whether or not I would have gotten a job with my college training, is irrelevant. The expanding of your awareness is the most valuable thing you will come away with from a college or university. I envy you, as young children. I am an old man. But I would love to do it all again. I would like to have a little of this perspective when doing it all again. Thank you.

MR. LI HONGSHENG

Li Hongsheng is the South China Region General Manager of RYB Education. He graduated from the Beijing Teaching University as an MD of Child Psychology. He has received the U.S. Erikson Advanced Early Childhood Master's Level Certification, an MD at the Montessori (Italy) National Engineering Institute, and was named International Tutor of Satya Family Therapy System. He is a nationally registered personal consultant and a senior nursery judge in Hunan, China.

An Assumption for Success -- Don't Use Your Current View to Plan Your Future

It is my pleasure to attend today's meeting. I'd like to share with you some of my life experiences from when I was young, which have had a big influence on my career.
I've been to more than twenty countries around the world, although I've dedicated most of my efforts on early childhood education. I have visited many universities as well since I want to know the impact that early childhood education differences have on the decision to pursue higher education.

My topic today is called "Assumed Success", which was first introduced by Harvard professor Amy Cuddy. She said that we should assume that we are successful until we finally make it. This idea gives me insights and makes me think a lot. Looking back to our parents' age, they used to teach us that we should use what we have to do what we can. For instance, if we have money, then we can think of buying a house. However, Dr. Amy Cuddy's idea brings me a brand new way of thinking: don't only view yourself in the future with your current vision. No matter if you are a high school student, applying for a university, or want to have your own business, you should first know what we want to do, then look for resources to make it happen.

When I was a teenager, I used to work in KFC. I was very skinny at that time. I was born when my parents were more than 50 years old, so when I entered into university, my parents were more than 70 years old. They couldn't work anymore and they were too poor to afford my tuition. I had to look for three part-time jobs outside the school and even then, I was still worrying about how could I buy a new jacket or where my next meal would come from. Since I was very small and skinny, nobody cared about me at that time. I didn't know how to play basketball or volleyball since I never had a chance to play with others. Compared to my fellow students who were from rich families, I felt very inferior. It took me a long time to regain confidence. At that time, I could never imagine that one day I would be able to stand here and give you this speech. As you can see, we should never view ourselves in the future with our current status; instead, we should think big, set a high goal when you are young, and figure out what you really want and work hard to achieve it.

I'm glad that there wasn't the internet at that time when I studied in university. I used my spare time to learn painting as well as play guitar and badminton. I didn't realize at that time what these kinds of "hobbies" could bring to me until I began to work. I found out that sports can strengthen our willpower, while drawing can enhance our sense of beauty. So, for me, adolescence was a period of preparation and practice.

This photo was taken when I graduated from university and it is the last photo of me with my parents, as shortly after my graduation, they passed away. My parents used to teach me that if you can suffer the insufferable, you are a breed above others; otherwise, you'll be beaten by life. Times are changing, but even so, our parents today should let their children know that we should learn from hardships to grow and be better, not just to endure and suffer from it.

I believe that everyone has potential; however, many parents struggle to see their children's potential right now because they haven't had much significant achievement yet. I'd like to introduce this book to you which was written by a high-school graduate. This conversation between a student and his teacher is very inspiring: "Teacher, I can't give a speech." "No, you just don't know how to give a speech *yet*." I hope that next time when your kid says to you "Mom, I can't do it", instead of blaming him, you change your words and say " No, you just don't know how to do it yet. "I believe these words will dramatically change the way of thinking of your kids, and encourage them to bring out the best of his or her potential.

I used to take a training course of Mr. Jack Ma Yun; he told us that in today's highly competitive times, we need to first figure out what we need to do, then learn how to do it. For instance, most high school students don't know what they want to do in the future. In reality, it doesn't really matter; all you need to do is try. Wondering will not get you anywhere. Only action can give you an answer. So, don't be afraid, just do it.

The last passage that I'd like to share with you is from this book, written by a former famous Taiwan singer called Chen Meilin. She had three sons and all of them were enrolled by Stanford University. The words I remembered most in her book was that she always told her sons, "when you are wondering how to make a decision, just remember to choose the more difficult one." It reminds me of one conversation between Harry Potter and his Headmaster Dumbledore. Dumbledore asked Harry Potter, "When you have options in life, what are they?" Harry Potter said, "The right way and the wrong way." The Headmaster said, "No. There is the right way and the easy way." Many of us tend to choose the easy way instead of the right way. However, if we try to always choose the harder way, the rest of our life's journey will become much easier.

HEADMASTER DAVE DELGADO

Mr. Delgado, a graduate of UC Berkeley, has 30 years of private school management experience including in various levels of administration, school development and organization, multi-campus accreditation, quality assurance, curriculum development, teacher selection and training, student assessment, student counseling, teaching, and problem-solving.

Study in the States

Thank you, HEARTS and hosts for your invitation and your hospitality. Well most people here study in the states for college or the great opportunities to attend some of the best colleges in the world, but international students are also an integral part of many high schools in the United States.

So to talk a little of the culture. For example, now, technology is progressing faster than ever, we can't even guess where it'll be in five or ten years from now. Jobs and careers exist today that we could not have even guessed or imagined ten to twenty years ago. Because of this, education and the culture surrounding it is evolving. We're currently preparing students for jobs that don't even exist using technologies that haven't been invented in order to solve problems we don't even know about yet. This evolution at focus on sciences and creative problem solving means that an even greater variety of choices in the curriculum.

Options, Opportunity, Availability – describe the education culture today. With the increased focus on science, technology, engineering, and mathematics, students have more options than ever in both the classes and electives. Today's high school student still has basic core classes to complete but even those have multiple options. A major characteristic of American schools is the high priority given to sports, clubs, and activities by the community, the parents, the schools, and the students themselves. These can be characterized as clubs, art, culture, language, student body government, school newspapers, volunteering. The United States spends more per student on education than any other country. With increased options and opportunities comes more things to choose, but with that freedom comes responsibility to choose, and choose wisely. To choose options that will lead you on a path to a successful and happy life.

Fortunately, many resources are available to American and international students on campus and off campus. Resources for students to help them do well in their academics subjects to selective classes, on their path to college, and to find a successful balance when selecting extracurricular activities. Some schools have been approved by the United States government to add international students to the mix. That's very fortunate for us because this provides tremendous benefit to everyone involved. On campus resources, such as counselors, faculty, advisors, are there to help students plan and coordinate their lives, prepping for standardized tests, AP honors courses so you can get that higher GPA, and sponsoring when you want to start a school club. International students are such an integral part of the student body that schools do everything they can to give any additional support, such as ESL classes, TOEFL testing, mixed or blended classrooms, many different things.

And, if that is not enough, off campus resources are available as well. Students who need more support than what's provided on campus don't need to look very far, cause the nature of off campus resources will arise to almost any situation. Libraries, learning centers, private tutors, prep classes, transportation services, and more. School administrators, such as myself, love seeing the American students with international students, as it helps mainstream international students so they're included in the school, community, and culture day to day. A great symbiotic relationship that enhances both their academic and social lives.

First, international students are an integral part of the academic life. Although international students study English, there's usually a gap when it comes to colloquial English and academic vocabulary, what they learn from school and what they learn from friends. When students meet international students who have left their own country, their home, their families, and their friends for education, they become inspired to appreciate their own education even more.

It's not just the academic life, international students are an integral part of the campus social life. I love seeing the learning in progress, any type of learning in progress. International students learn the American culture from their new friends. They share music, they go to sports events and dances and parties and the malls, the movies, and American students learn more about other cultures from their new friends than they could from any book.

Also very important, is that these students are building bridges between cultures for future generations. Just imagine later in life, you go on a business trip to China or Vietnam, or America or Germany or India, and you already have a friend there, and an understanding of the culture there. As Franklin Roosevelt stated, democracy cannot succeed unless those who express their choice are prepared to choose wisely. The real safeguard of democracy, therefore, is education. And, as I will mention later, education is also the safeguard of our entire planet's limited resources. The students who come from any country to study in the States, especially at these young ages. There was a point in time when our student population increased faster than our ability to find hosts for them, so my family began taking in students from China, but there was this girl who arrived, she was only twelve years old. Families value education so much that they're willing to send their twelve year old child to another country, to live with strangers, to get a good education. And I don't know how to explain it any more, but that's very appreciated by an educator.

I'd like to show and share with you some of the success stories that I've seen from students, from highschool to thinking about preparing for their path and going to college, and there's a person here who looks just like you, maybe you thought, 'I don't know if I'll make it in the States, I don't know if I'll make it in another school, I have the entrance exams in a couple days, what do I do?'. There are possibilities and options in the States for highschool students to prepare for college, even if you thought maybe you weren't ready for college. So, I'm going to share a couple of success stories.

First, there's Cassie: she attended high school in the US for two years, lived with an English speaking host family, she took a couple of AP Courses, along with her full course load, she chose a surprising elective- motorsports, she joined an Interact Club and learned to love community service, and she was able to visit colleges before making her final choice. She graduated from UC Irvine with a double major in only three years with an Order of Merit Award, Chancellor's Award of Distinction, Phi Beta Kappa, this September, she enters the graduate program at Stanford University that only accepted 20 students total. The goal of her research, her publications is to help Chinese students with the cultural adjustment, so they can be more successful in college. Its a study of international education. And, Cassie is here with me today in her hometown of Wuhan.

There's Randy, he attended highschool in the US for three years, his parents were certain his grades weren't high enough to get into the University of California, but he visited the UC campuses, learned more about them, he learned that they consider other factors besides grades. His friendships with American students rapidly increased his English proficiency and sense of humor, he studied with American teachers and students to improve his standardized test scores, he earned his way into the National Honor Society, he received admission offers from UCSC Computer Science, UC Riverside, Cal Poly, San Jose State, Ohio State, and more. He will be attending UC Davis this fall studying mathematics.

There's another type of student, Sabrina, she's a go-getter. She came to the US and completed all highschool requirements in only three years. She's valedictorian of her class, joined the Interact Club, became president, learned to love community service, taught others to love it, she earned her way into the National Honor Society, took advantage of local resources, did a local internship, and received admission offers from St. John's University, Temple, UC Merced, California Lutheran, Hobart William Smith, Union College King's College, all with generous scholarship offers. She will be attending University of California, Santa Cruz on a $30,000 Dean's Scholarship Award. UC's usually don't give out scholarships to international students. So, to stay on time, there are many more here, there was a student who came with the lowest TOEFL score I've seen, but she's going to UCSC.

There was another student who wasn't even expecting to make it into college, he got college offers and scholarships. There are many more success stories, students who came to the US, studied and got into college, and you will find one of them at least, that is just like you. Thank you everyone.

KEVIN BRYAN

I am a student in the 11th grade at Junipero Serra High School, an all-boys school in the Bay Area of California. I am particularly interested in science and mathematics, focusing on courses in AP Biology, AP Physics C, AP Chemistry, and AP Calculus, as well as internships at Stanford and UCSF. I am involved in a variety of extra-curricular activities in and out of school. I play classical and jazz piano, highlighted by my participation in my school's award-winning jazz ensemble. I row for my school's crew team, where I compete in races against some of the top teams in America. I also enjoy being President of the Serra Science Club and the National Honor Society as well as editor in chief for Tempus Magazine.

Jazz in American Schools

Jazz is a musical art form that both reflects and influences American history and continues to make a mark on students throughout the nation.

Jazz first arose during the early 20th century in New Orleans, Louisiana, but is rooted in African and European musical traditions. Many musical influences such as Spanish folk music, French band music, ragtime, and the blues made an impact on American jazz. A tribute to the immense importance of jazz in American history, the 1920s are often called the "Jazz Age" of U.S. history, a time when the style found enormous popularity. During this time, famous musicians such as Louis Armstrong and Duke Ellington made their claim to fame. In the 1930s, swing jazz became more prevalent, where larger bands were more often utilized, but still allowing the players to find room for creativity and individuality. During the 1940s and beyond, other influences from Latin American and African countries led to new styles including Latin Jazz, Cool Jazz, and Bebop.

Jazz is a unique art form that integrates the common format of music with its own special qualities. The music was originally passed down by ear instead of through written sheet music, which allowed for flexibility in how each piece could be played. Jazz has all the components that other music has: melody, harmony, rhythm. Improvisation is one of the hallmarks of jazz. Soloing allows players to express their ideas and emotions through their instruments. In larger bands, these solos can play off the rhythms that other band members introduce, which leaves a lot of room for creativity.

While Jazz has seen a decline in the top charts of the music industry, it has seen an explosive rise in schools across America. Jazz education has nearly quadrupled in the last 50 years, and it is unusual for a school not to have a jazz ensemble. Students now have unprecedented amounts of resources to better their understanding of Jazz. Students not only can attend concerts, clinics, and workshops provided in their schools to hone their skills and techniques, but they also can expose themselves to the playing of Jazz music greats such as Count Basie, Duke Ellington, and Dave Brubeck through a quick internet search.

Jazz is a superb extracurricular builder that is rewarding and enjoyable. Every school day, I have a jazz class for one hour starting at 7 a.m. before my other classes begin. Since starting jazz, I have seen a multitude of benefits to myself. Playing jazz is a great and energizing way to start the day. You learn to be a team player as well as to develop your own identity as a musician. Jazz is also a notable extracurricular activity that college admissions keep an eye out for. Many top schools including the Juilliard School, Columbia University, Johns Hopkins University, and Northwestern all have top jazz programs that students attend every year.

Jazz has become more than just an American music style. Every major city in the world now has a first-rate home grown-jazz talent, local performance venues, and knowledgeable fans. Jazz has spread to China through a style called "Shidaiqu", which is a type of Chinese folk music and American jazz fusion that found its beginnings in Shanghai. Bai Hong, Bai Guang, Zhou Xuan, and Gong Qiuxia are all notable Chinese jazz artists who have led to rising interest in Chinese jazz. Modern movies such as the extremely successful "Crazy Rich Asians" has also led to greater exposure of jazz to more people throughout the world.

If you learn one thing from my presentation today, I hope it is what benefits jazz can bring to you. It is also my hope that some of the audience today will now attempt to pursue jazz on their own. Thank you for listening.

JENNY WANG

Jenny Wang is a junior at Flintridge Sacred Heart Academy in Los Angeles. She came to the United States to study in September 2017. She loves discussing literature and history, as well as learning about the development of societies and cultures of different countries. At school, she has joined the Speech & Debate club to express her opinions on problems in our society. In her spare time, she likes to play golf and attend various golf tournaments. She also enjoys travel with her family and uses her camera to record her life journey.

Vintage and Retro:

I often feel like I am a very vintage person, because I am especially interested in the styles that were in the past. So today I want to share with you my perspective on vintage. First of all, what is Vintage? Vintage is usually a retro feeling. It is a unique memory people have for one of the items in previous generations. Changes in society have prompted this feeling of retro, making people become reminiscent and nostalgic. However, sometimes the difference between vintage and retro is hard to distinguish the differences. Retro is an emotion, while vintage is a style, and people who love vintage normally have an attitude that goes along with their likings.

Vintage clothing and fashion have become very popular. Looking over the fashion history of the 20th Century, it is not hard to see that there is a very stand out style that represents each time period. In the 1920s, we had formal suits and suit dresses. Moving into the 40s, many preferred good looking army uniforms; they were very popular after World War II. In the 60s, we had Hippie and Bohemian styles of clothes. Finally, we had jeans in the 80s and 90s, which still remain popular in today's society.

Last but not least, I would like to share a story with you all. It was a hot summer and I was walking down the streets with my grandmother in downtown Shanghai. An old lady stopped us and asked if we wanted to buy her flowers. I ignored her and walked straight past, but I realized my grandmother did not follow my steps. Turning back, I saw her talking with the old lady with a concentrated face, not realizing I already left. I thought it was useless that she decided to buy the flowers, but it turned out that I was completely wrong. The flower that old lady sold was not something usual, but actually an item from my grandmother's childhood. That flower is called Michelia alba, the city flower of Shanghai, and it signifies innocent love and sincere friendship, Not many people actually know about this flower. They were once very popular during my grandmother's and even my mother's generation, but not very well known at my age. Probably because of the fast development in Shanghai into a modernized city and the great migration from other cities and countries, the city was losing its unique cultural characteristics and becoming more international. This flower lost its popularity over time, and not many people living in Shanghai recognize its significance. The old lady found resonance with my grandma's childhood and actually decided to give these flowers to us for free. She pinned the flower on my clothes near my chest and helped me to wear the flower bracelet she made. She told me that the girl who wears this flower is virtuous and beautiful, with special personality that others don't have. She also told us she was selling the flowers, not for any income, but for her own pleasure and to preserve Shanghai culture. She would be satisfied even if there were a couple of people who came to her and recognized the beauty of the flower. I was touched by the old lady's spirit in sharing the culture of this flower. I began to feel personally attached to my Shanghai heritage, and my willingness to preserve my culture has increased.

Not many of the new generation in Shanghai care about our cultural heritage. Growing up in Shanghai, I didn't understand the inside meaning of being a Shanghainese. I refused to speak the native Shanghai dialect, and my English is actually better than my Shanghainese. However, after this experience, my Shanghai heritage had awoken, turning me into someone who cared about my own culture, and eager to explore the meaning behind my identity. I want to preserve the stories and uniqueness of my cultural heritage. I want to capture the beauty of michelia alba, and spread it to more people, keeping it an everlasting flower in people's heart that will never fade.

SERENA MAO

Serena is a rising junior at Mission San Jose High School. She competes in her high school debate team and participates in an all-girls robotics team. She also likes to experiment and create new things through arts and programming. In her free time, she enjoys dancing, hanging out with friends, and listening to music

Stress and How to Deal

Stress in schools is one of the biggest contributors to teens' health in today's world. The epitome of stress can be witnessed in Chinese schools. The Educational Review concludes that students in China feel disproportionately more stress than others around the world. On the other hand, although it is comparatively less widespread, Americans are similarly busy and stressed in their workplace or school environments. The US-China Education Review published a study in 2017 analyzing the differences and similarities between stress in Chinese and American high schools. It found that Chinese students tended to spend more time on schoolwork, and less time playing sports and sleeping than American students. However, even though the time distribution is different between the two countries, academic stress within the student population is roughly equal.

Clearly, both countries experience a very high-pressure environment daily. And the fact that it's everywhere becomes a problem because nobody likes to be stressed out. It's not something people enjoy feeling. Hating stress is justified, as the Mayo Clinic explains that excessive stress can cause illness, insomnia, decreased productivity, and a list of other negative effects that just goes on and on. As you might expect, there are numerous internet articles, magazines, and books to help with this pervasive phenomenon. But what is the solution? Exercise? Tai Chi? Laughter? Aside from the various other things, you can attempt to reduce stress by merely changing your perception of stress, which can be a game-changer.

Yes, stress can hurt you both physically and mentally. But demonizing it and turning it into the enemy may not be the solution. The University of Wisconsin researchers tracked 30,000 American adults for eight years, finding that those who reported feeling a significant amount of stress were 43% more likely to die. But there's a catch. The higher death rates only affected those who thought of stress as bad. On the other hand, people with a positive view of stress had among the lowest death rates in the group, even lower than those who didn't experience much stress. This negative view of stress can be a silent killer, as a wider application of the study reveals that thinking of stress as bad causes 20,000 American deaths a year. That would make it the 15th highest cause of death in the US.

But how exactly are we supposed to see stress as good? When you're conventionally stressed, there's a rush of adrenaline, your heart beats faster, you breathe more frequently, and you might start sweating. Typically, we see this as a sign that our body can't cope properly with stress. But when participants of a study at Harvard University were told that stress was an energizing force preparing them to face the challenge, things changed for the better. They performed much better in purposely stress-inducing experiments. But apart from the more obvious results, the more physical responses to stress also improved. Blood vessels typically constrict when you are under stress, thus heightening the risk of cardiovascular disease. Interestingly, those who saw stress as beneficial did not see their blood vessels constrict while others still did.

So the next time you're stressed, take a step back and reevaluate your approach. Try not to be so stressed about stress. Instead, see it as your body's way of preparing you for the challenges ahead, and that belief might very well come true.

WILL (PEIHONG) WU

Will Wu is a junior at Valley Christian High school. He has loved music since his childhood, especially music composition. He has composed several pieces on his own. He also loves psychology and traditional culture. He loves spending time learning about ancient culture and humanity. In his spare time, he likes to compose music and play basketball.

Music: A Process of Creation

What is music? How do people now define music? By searching online and in a dictionary, I found out that the definition of music is an art of sound in time that expresses ideas and emotions in significant forms through the elements of rhythm, melody, harmony, and color. However, That is what I call "the general view of music" or " public view on music", in other words, for myself I have a different definition. My definition of music is a form of creativity.

I believed that many people have heard those terms like " melody", " harmony" and " rhythm" which are basic parts of music. For instance, in the most basic composition process, people create a melody, think through how to harmonize it and decide to play in what rhythm. This sounds like a math equation - just plug in this and get music. But think about the process. How do people come up with a melody line? Is it coming from the middle of nowhere? And how do people know to harmonize the melody and to know what rhythm they are going to use? Maybe you can say people could learn this from music theory and past experiences, which are elements that can't be denied. However, there is a role for creativity, which leads people to plot the melody with harmony and rhythms the way the do. Because music theory hasn't changed over many years, people need to have the creativity to make new beautiful songs from the rigid function. Brainstorming is a process to get a musical idea, so past experiences can help people with the creative process. But nothing can replace creativity.

We just discussed the general composition which requires creative input, but now we are about to look at the musical pieces. Transitions and cadences are two difficult parts of composition. There are different ways to create a transition. I learned that the most simple transition was the sudden transition (abrupt modulation). This creates no transition, just directly changes the style, the key, and the tempo. But this method could not be used in all situations. Most of the time, we want to use a pivot chord modulation which enables a smooth change from one key to another. A pivot chord is a chord that belongs both the home key and the key the music is changing to. People who learn music theory know about both these ways of modulation. But how to use those modulations in a creative way is always a problem. So the transition part needs people's creativity to find a comfortable or appropriate way to not only transfer the music smoothly but also to make the listener feel satisfied and or even amazed. The other part is cadencing which is the ending of a music piece. There are different kinds of cadences. It contains two big categories depending on whether the last chord ends on the tonic or not: finished cadences and unfinished cadences. Furthermore, finished cadences include the authentic cadence and plagal cadence. On the other side, unfinished cadences include imperfect and interrupted/deceptive cadence. How could people lead their music pieces to those fixed ending? Why do different composers have hundreds of ways to lead toward those four types of endings? It is all because they have creativity which helps them to invent an innovative way to end the music.

To sum up, creativity is an indispensable part of music, even though we might need experience as well. Creativity helps us to make music unique. Lastly, creativity gives us the vision to create new types of music. That is why I call music a form of creativity.

EILEEN GUO

Eileen Guo is a sophomore at Gunn High School. She enjoys doing taekwondo, volunteering, painting, and learning new languages. She has earned her second-degree black belt in taekwondo, a sport that she has been very passionate about and practiced over the past 7 years. Eileen also loves art. She loves to draw during her free time, and has produced a few award-winning paintings!

Visual Arts

Visual and performing arts are an essential part of the American education system. I've been interested in arts my whole life and recently started immersing much of my time in drawing, painting, graphic design, and video production.

Walking into a class full of techy upperclassmen as a freshman, on the first day of school was so overwhelming. I had no idea how to run a live broadcasted show, no idea what shutter speed or aperture was, nor did I know how to edit on any kind of software. I was starting on base one, when everyone else knew how to work the equipment, knew their fellow classmates, and had already built a great rapport with the teacher. Me, on the other hand, knew no one and nothing. Slowly but surely, I started raising my hand during class discussions, I decided to take leadership roles in filming and script-writing with the support from upperclassmen. Going out during lunch to film interviews, and holding a camera just gave me a strange sense of power. I was able to capture and tell the stories that have yet been told. I received so much help from my teacher and other classmates, and soon, my first video was finished! All the hours spent planning the video idea, scheduling an interview, checking out equipment, filming, and editing finally paid off; not really-- I watched videos that my fellow classmates had made, and looked online at professional videographers' videos and realized my video was so terrible. But I had set my mind to it; I had deeply fallen in love with video production and was determined to improve. The following year (this year), my teacher asked me to be the lead videographer and lifestyle producer of my own content group. I was ecstatic; it was time for me to teach others the skills that I had learned and share the love for this subject I have. My lifestyle group and I have built an inseparable bond and I'm so glad that we've gotten to learn more, together throughout this year.

Outside of school, I also do drawing and painting. For years and years, I used pencil, watercolor, pastel, chalk, clay, to create art, that by the standards of my teacher, were never good enough. It was extremely disappointing: so much time and effort, and no visible improvement. I transferred to another teacher who would basically neglect many of his students, and we had to sit on an uncomfortable wooden bench for three hours, drawing a sphere with a dull piece of charcoal. I thought that this was even worse than my past art classes. After going to these classes for a few years, I suddenly sparked; drawing became easier and more enjoyable. Quickly, I moved from charcoal to oil painting. The splashes of color on a canvas made me so happy. From still-life, I moved on to landscape, and then to portrait. I love going to art to learn more and see my pieces come to life, week after week.

Drawing and painting can be seen as more of a traditional, old-fashioned form of visual arts. With the quick, technological progressions happening in our world, I thought that graphic design would give me a new insight into a contemporary form of art. Just in the past few months, I've gotten to learn how to use Photoshop, InDesign, Illustrator, and much more software I had never even heard of. We've gotten to make our school posters, different logos, our own fonts, and stickers! Not only is getting to learn a new art form exhilarating, but the community I've gotten to know is also amazing. I've gotten to build a great rapport with my teacher, and he helps me think of ideas, not only for digital designs, but also names for my paintings, or ideas for new pieces that I'm creating. I've built friendships with talented upperclassmen who bring so much joy into every class period, and most importantly, learned a new art form that I'll be able to use forever.

All these forms of visual art have sparked new joys, taught me new lessons, and have opened up countless opportunities in my life.

ANDY (YUHAO) WANG

Andy Wang is an international student, a junior of Valley Christian School in Dublin. His favorite subject is drawing, especially in the concept design of characters. Drawing is also the major subject he is going to study at college. He also participates in some sports, such as tennis, soccer, swimming, and football.

The Importance of Visual and Performing Arts for Students in the 21st Century

Hi everyone, my name is Andy Wang. The topic I am going to talk about is the importance of learning visual and performing arts.

First, I want to define what visual and performing arts are. Visual arts, such as drawing, graphics, painting, sculpture, and decoration, are created primarily for visual perception. In contrast, the performing arts are a form of art in which artists use their voices, bodies, or inanimate objects to convey artistic expression. Arts education refers to education in the disciplines of music, dance, theatre, and visual arts.

Next, I am going to talk about the importance of learning visual and performing arts. Arts education is an integral part of the development of each individual. The philosopher Plato and many others have emphasized the importance of the arts in the education process. Working in the arts helps learners to develop creative problem-solving skills. Visual arts teach people about color, layout, perspective, and balance, which are all techniques that are necessary for the presentation (visual, digital) of academic work. Studying performing arts helps students to develop critical reflection, collaboration, creativity, and communication. Students gain valuable life skills by learning the importance of feedback, both positive and constructive. Performing arts is a discipline that encourages teamwork, whether that is in writing, creating, or performing. Through creative expression, students learn to understand the world in a unique way, preparing them to navigate the challenges after finishing school.

Communication skills can be improved through performing arts, as students learn to use verbal and non-verbal techniques in new ways to deliver their message. Arts experiences boost critical thinking, teaching students to take time to be more careful and thorough in how they observe the world. A report by Americans for the Arts states that young people who participate regularly in the arts are four times more likely to be recognized for academic achievement, to participate in a math and science fair, or to win an award for writing an essay or poem compared to children who do not participate.

In conclusion, the importance of visual and performing arts in education cannot be overstated. It is proven that students with arts education are more successful than those without it.

PETER (ZERU) LI

Peter Li is an incoming sophomore at Saratoga High School. He likes to read books, especially historical and mystery novels. Peter is a clarinet player in the Saratoga High School band, and he enjoys his time in the marching band. During his free time, he likes to play the clarinet, read books, and take photographs.

Differences in Education Between China and the U.S.

Hi, I'm Peter Li, and I study at a high school in the United States. Today I would like to share my experiences and thoughts on the differences between Chinese and American K-12 education systems. In the past 15 years, I've attended many different schools, including schools both in China and the United States. I studied in China from kindergarten to 5th grade, then I moved to Irvine, California for 6th and 7th grade. Due to my parents' career relocation, my family and I had to move back to China during my 8th grade, and now I'm a freshman at Saratoga High School in the San Francisco Bay Area. The differences that stand out to me the most are testing, socialization, individualized thinking, and hands-on learning.

First of all, even though testing plays an important role in both education systems, there is a difference in how testing is used for college admissions. In the United States, your grade point average is more important than certain test scores. However, there is no such thing as grade point average in most Chinese schools. Grades for the whole school year are determined by the semester finals scores. Most Chinese people have a misconception that SAT or ACT is as important as the Chinese "Gaokao", which is a Chinese standardized test that is required of high schoolers to be admitted into higher education. In reality, these test scores are considered supplementary to grade point average, and their importance is less than that of the grade point average.

Now let's move on to the differences in classrooms. In the United States, students go to different classrooms for each of their classes. Making friends in U.S. schools oftentimes takes place outside the classroom. Students may choose who they want to make friends with and their friends don't need to be in the same class. For example, students at my school chat and discuss with their friends at the library. Whereas in China, students are stationed in their homeroom, and different teachers come to the class. Students in China study and sit with the same classmates every day. Students in the same class become friends naturally without any pressure because their friends are practically chosen for them. Students in the same class have a closer bond with their classmates because they are familiar with whoever sits next to them.

In regards to individualized thinking, the two education systems are at odds with each other. Students in the United States are given more freedom in thinking creatively whereas students in China are taught to memorize the correct answers to questions. In the U.S., students are encouraged to think critically and to question their teachers. In my math class, a student told our math teacher that the teacher's answer was wrong. Indeed, the teacher got the answer wrong but didn't get upset when the student challenged her authority. In contrast, students in China are taught to obey their teachers and not to question their teachers at any time. For instance, one of my friends in my Chinese middle school asked our teacher a question about a piece of history and was told that there could only be one interpretation. The teacher was a little bit upset because someone dared to challenge him. The whole class was a bit shocked when it heard that there was only one right answer to the question. Students in the United States are given more freedom in class to elaborate on thinkings whereas students in China apply their knowledge to questions.

Lastly, learning activities is also very different between the two systems. In the United States, students have more in-class activities where they interact with each other because they are encouraged to learn things from actions. It is more important for students in the United States to learn things through hands-on activities than getting good scores. For example, we do a lot of labs in Biology in the United States such as a pig dissection. In China, there are only a few hands-on activities in the whole school year, and students learn things mostly from reading textbooks. It is more important to score high on the exams than to really understand the concept through concrete activities. For instance, in my Chinese middle school, we did Biology workbooks every day instead of hands-on activities.

In conclusion, education between the two countries are quite different, and the major differences are testing, socialization, individualized thinking, and hands-on learning. Hopefully, in the future, the two systems can learn more from each other and improve themselves.

YUKIKO (ZHUOTONG) XIAN

Yukiko Xian is an 18-year-old student from China. She is studying at Los Gatos High School. She has participated in many activities such as Youth International Environment Protection Awareness and HEARTS. She also is a leader of the iCare Club.

High School Student Community Service and Tibet Project

Today, I would like to introduce to you the importance of community service to American high school students. Many high school students in the United States are required to complete a certain number of community service hours every year which are necessary before graduation. My school requires us to complete 50 hours of community service every year. The school provides the students with many types of jobs that count for service hours, including assisting teachers, teaching lower-grade students, sorting books in the library, or even helping children in Africa. For American high school students, having an adequate number of community service hours has a crucial influence on college applications. These extracurricular activities enable students to have better contact with society and the world, as well as enriching their lives beyond their school education. In my case, I have been working as a volunteer in a special needs agency. I accompany the children and do activities with them such as singing and dancing. When I see this group of lovely and innocent children, who are different due to their mental disabilities, I became a little more enlightened about the situations of these students. Even though I do not stay with them for very long, going to visit them is a wonderful experience.

Next, let's talk a little about teaching, which I have just finished at the Mingyue Hope Primary School in the Tibetan Autonomous region of Sichuan and Tibet. In this remote Qinghai-Tibet Plateau, there is a large temperature difference between day and night, harsh weather, and limited resources for education, medicine, and transportation. Most children we are helping are orphans and live in isolated mountain areas with few families nearby. Occasionally volunteers come to make generous contributions to the children. In this kind of environment, these children must grow adaptively. When we become familiar with the children, we can start to notice traces of their past tribulations. However, they still choose kindness and trust. Although I live in the United States, far from these children, I still want to do something to make their lives better. For example, I want to make medicine available to them when they are sick. I want them to know that the world embraces them with open arms and that they are not abandoned. I want them to know that there are people in this world who love them. When those children are trying their best to live, how can we not do our best to help them?

Community service allows us to understand the world better. I hope you can join us to help those in need!

DEREK DONG

Derek Dong is about to attend his Senior year at Palo Alto High School. He loves reading, especially about history and non-fiction. He also enjoys physical activity, mainly sports, and has played for both the school basketball team and football team. Derek is also a successful coach, leading the Jordan Middle School 7th and 6th grade basketball teams to the playoffs. In his spare time, Derek Dong enjoys reading, engaging in physical activity, whether that be sports or weight lifting, or trying new foods or cuisines.

Popular Books in the US and China

First, I would like to talk about Chinese books.

1. San Guo Yan Yi

    The story – part historical, part legend, and part mythical – romanticizes and dramatizes the lives of feudal lords and their retainers, who tried to replace the dwindling Han dynasty or restore it. While the novel follows hundreds of characters, the focus is mainly on the three power blocs that emerged from the remnants of the Han dynasty, and would eventually form the three states of Cao Wei, Shu Han, and Eastern Wu. The novel deals with the plots, personal and military battles, intrigues, and struggles of these states to achieve dominance for almost 100 years.

2. Shui Hu Zhuan

    The story, set in the Song dynasty, tells of how a group of 108 outlaws gather at Mount Liang (or Liangshan Marsh) to form a sizable army before they are eventually granted amnesty by the government and sent on campaigns to resist foreign invaders and suppress rebel forces.

3. Xi You Ji

The novel is an extended account of the legendary pilgrimage of the Tang dynasty Buddhist monk Xuanzang who traveled to the "Western Regions", that is, Central Asia and India, to obtain Buddhist sacred texts (sūtras) and returned after many trials and much suffering. It retains the broad outline of Xuanzang's own account, *Great Tang Records on the Western Regions*, but the Ming dynasty novel adds elements from folk tales and the author's invention, that is, that Gautama Buddha gave this task to the monk (referred to as Tang Sanzang in the novel) and provided him with three protectors who agree to help him as an atonement for their sins. These disciples are Sun Wukong, Zhu Bajie, and Sha Wujing, together with a dragon prince who acts as Tang Sanzang's steed, a white horse.

4. Hong Lou Meng

Red Chamber is believed to be semi-autobiographical, mirroring the rise and decline of author Cao Xueqin's own family and, by extension, of the Qing dynasty.[4] As the author details in the first chapter, it is intended to be a memorial to the damsels he knew in his youth: friends, relatives, and servants. The novel is remarkable not only for its huge cast of characters and psychological scope but also for its precise and detailed observation of the life and social structures typical of 18th-century Chinese society.

Now, let's see some famous western books.

1. Beowulf - 10th Century - "The Beowulf Poet"

The story is set in Scandinavia. Beowulf, a hero of the Geats, comes to the aid of Hrothgar, the king of the Danes, whose mead hall in Heorot has been under attack by a monster known as Grendel. After Beowulf slays him, Grendel's mother attacks the hall and is then also defeated. Victorious, Beowulf goes home to Geatland and later becomes king of the Geats. After a period of fifty years has passed, Beowulf defeats a dragon, but is mortally wounded in the battle. After his death, his attendants cremate his body and erect a tower on a headland in his memory.

2. Romeo and Juliet - 16th Century - Shakespeare

   Romeo and Juliet is a tragedy written by William Shakespeare early in his career about two young star-crossed lovers whose deaths ultimately reconcile their feuding families. It was among Shakespeare's most popular plays during his lifetime and along with *Hamlet*, is one of his most frequently performed plays. Today, the title characters are regarded as archetypal young lovers.

3. Pride and Prejudice - 19th Century - Jane Austen

   Mr. Bennet of the Longbourn estate has five daughters, but his property is inalienable intact entailed by a fee tail male, meaning that none of the girls can inherit it. His wife has no fortune, so it is imperative that at least one of the girls marry well to support the others upon his death. Jane Austen's opening line, "It is a truth universally acknowledged, that a single man in possession of a good fortune, must be in want of a wife", is a sentence filled with irony and playfulness. The novel revolves around the importance of marrying for love, not simply for money, despite the social pressures to make a good (i.e., wealthy) match.

4. The Lord of the Rings - 20th Century - J.R.R. Tolkien

   The title of the novel refers to the story's main antagonist, the Dark Lord Sauron, who had in an earlier age created the One Ring to rule the other Rings of Power as the ultimate weapon in his campaign to conquer and rule all of Middle-earth. From quiet beginnings in the Shire, a hobbit land not unlike the English countryside, the story ranges across Middle-earth, following the course of the War of the Ring through the eyes of its characters, not only the hobbits Frodo Baggins, Samwise "Sam" Gamgee, Meriadoc "Merry" Brandybuck and Peregrin "Pippin" Took, but also the hobbits' chief allies and travelling companions: the Men, Aragorn, a Ranger of the North, and Boromir, a Captain of Gondor; Gimli, a Dwarf warrior; Legolas Greenleaf, an Elven prince; and Gandalf, a wizard.

As we can see, Chinese and western books have many similarities and differences. Thank you.

2019 Youth International Environment Protection Awareness Conference

2019
Youth International Environment Protection Awareness Conference

Location: Wuhan, China; Date: June 23, 2019
Hosts of Conference: Kevin Bryan and Jenny Wang
Interpreters for Guest Speakers: Eileen Guo, Serena Mao, Jenny Wang, Zeru Peter Li, Will Wu

This has been the fifth annual Youth International Environment Protection Awareness Conference. The purpose is to have professionals and students exchange information and ideas about what we can do to help the environment. We have translated, transcribed, compiled, and edited the speeches of all our speakers.

Proceeding Editors: Derek Dong, Kevin Bryan

DR. JAY JONES, PHD

Professor Jones has a broad academic background, with concentrations in Botany, Microbiology, Chemistry and Geology. His research and work experience includes: Senior Research Geobotanist, conducting research on oil and gas exploration (ARCO), Naturalist/ Interpreter (National Park Service), Remote Sensing Consultant (NASA/Lockheed). He is at home in the field conducting floral surveys, as well as in the laboratory working with complex analytical instrumentation. As Professor of Biology and Biochemistry, Jay has taught an exceptionally broad range of courses including versions of an interdisciplinary course entitled: Toward a Sustainable Planet. Many of these courses have field components in which faculty and students see the global impact of the human species in various countries around the world. His current focus is on finding transdisciplinary paths toward sustainability.

How to Live Sustainably in an Environmentally Challenged World

Thank you for that kind introduction and for the opportunity to address this important issue.

There are many books, articles, and talks given on environmental topics. So many that we become numb to their content.

Most people realize environmental problems exist but few in the developed world realize how serious and how urgent these problems are.

Therefore, I approach this talk with a sense of responsibility to not only share basic information, but to touch the hearts of those gathered here so that we may work together to take action and reduce the impact of our species.

The current trends in the world are not encouraging. We are separated from each other and from the natural system upon which we and future generations depend. However, there is hope and we can achieve an even better way of life while improving the environment.

Earth is home to us all: Our families, friends, and neighbors – Every human being. It is also home to all other known living organisms.

This is where we all live along with all known life forms.

This seems very large and from the perspective of an individual it seems like it would be impossible to damage the whole environment.

But although the Earth is vast. All living organisms live within a few miles of the earth's surface and the vast majority of humans reside within one vertical mile of sea level. We call this thin layer the Biosphere.

If we compare a cross section of an apple to the earth, the biosphere would be thinner than the skin of the apple. Still there is a lot of room on the earth's surface and it takes many humans to cause significant harm.

Most of us are aware that we are affecting the environment and that serious problems exist. The reason for this can be seen in this famous image of the earth at night. Each bright area is a city or other center of human activity. This well known NASA satellite composite was produced in the year 2000. Today it would even be brighter, with the growth of cities in size and number.

In 2000 the world population was about 6 billion. We have added more than 1.3 billion more people in the 15 years since.

So what is the current state of the world?

- Human population has skyrocketed
- Scientific technology has allowed humans to greatly affect the environment and our ecological footprint
- We are using more resources than the Earth can sustainably provide
- We are also damaging its ability to sustain us through development and misuse
- The current course is not sustainable. We must change our ways.

It took 125 years to double the population from 1 billion in 1804 to 2 billion in 1927. It only took 13 years to add an equivalent amount since 2000.

We expect to have over 9 billion by 2050.

Science and technology has given us the ability to harness free energy and to create many synthetic products. As a result we have made enormous changes and produced many materials that cannot be accommodated in natural environments. Plastics are a good example, and they are accumulating across the land and in our oceans.

Technology has given us the ability to use the earth's resources faster than the earth can replace them.

We started using more than the earth produced around 1980.

Today we use about 1.4 x the earth's productivity.

We are depleting the earth's reserves, just as a checking account balance declines when one withdraws more than one deposits. This cannot go on for long because we are depleting the reserves at an increasing rate.

At the same time we are damaging the earth's ability to provide the resources we depend on.

Air pollution is one of the effects of our activity. Many of us live in areas with severe air pollution. It not only damages our health and deteriorates buildings and goods, but it also damages plants so that they are less able to clean the air and produce the food and oxygen upon which we depend.

Shanghai is one of those places but many rural areas also suffer from poor air quality because of mining or agricultural practices.

This dramatic photo shows enormous piles of coal. One of the major sources of air, water and soil pollution.

Producing and burning petroleum is another major source of pollution.

Heavy metals such as lead, mercury and cadmium are concentrated in coal and are released when it is burned. Most of the mercury in the marine food chain comes from coal fired power plants.

Coal fired power plant emissions can also contain significant amounts of radioactive nuclides.

We have all seen examples of severe water pollution. The upper left is one of the places on the Los Angeles river where the floating trash collects.

The one on the right is near Dublin, Ireland.

And the bottom left image illustrates fish kill due to agricultural runoff.

> Dead zones in coastal waters
> Coral reef deterioration
> Groundwater and aquifer contamination
> Loss of estuaries to development and pollution

Accumulation of organic pollutants, e.g. pharmaceuticals, pesticides, herbicides, heavy metals.

> Salinization
> Plasticizers . . .

Think bottled water is a good option? Sometimes.

But in our laboratory we have extracted PET plastic water bottles and found significant amounts of extractable phthalates, which causes numerous health issues.

Air, water, and soil pollutants travel around the world. Twenty five percent of airborne particulates in Los Angeles on some days, originate in China.

You have probably heard of the oceanic garbage patches in the five gyres. Plastic from around the world get circulated and end up on beaches and accumulating in massive quantities in the oceans. These toys released by accident over 20 years ago have now been distributed around the world.

And we have also seen examples of the destruction of land habitats by mining, development and agriculture.

We are removing natural vegetation and habitat for mining, housing, agriculture, dumps, highways and other developments at an ever increasing rate.

The upper right is a view from the Athabasca Tar Sands one of the world's worst ecological nightmares.

Pesticides and herbicides disrupt soil biota further damaging the ecosystem

Mining, industrial agriculture, construction, roads, airports . . .

The animals and plants that once lived in these areas have no place to go.

The image on the left is a photo of the tallgrass prairie of North America. Over 98% of this habitat has been developed, mostly for agriculture. The image in the upper left shows circular green fields of alfalfa, grown to feed dairy cattle in the facilities shown by the arrows.

The image below that is one of many enormous piles of bison skulls created in the 19th century when these inhabitants of the tallgrass prairie were killed by the millions.

Deforestation is another example of the destruction of ecosystems to meet our needs and wants.

The plants and animals that lived there are exterminated to plant soybeans, sugarcane, maize, canola, coffee or other industrial agricultural products.

Intense industrial agriculture imbalances ecosystems causing air and water pollution.

One might also question the ethics of treating animals. I return to the fact that we are separated from the system upon which we depend. Few of us have experienced the stench and immoral conditions that are used to raise the chicken that we eat. We must reconnect. Chickens have personalities. Those of you that have raised them know this. Once you reconnect you will find it hard to buy or eat chicken that you know were raised under these conditions. To buy or eat chicken raised this way is voting for this practice.

Most swine are raised industrially now in a fashion similar to poultry. The average swine farm in the US has approximately 40,000 hogs. We would never treat our pets in this fashion.

The rectangular pool in the upper left contains massive volumes of excrement, which contaminates the surface and groundwater.

An increasing number of our vegetables are now grown by intense industrial methods with loss of genetic diversity and often sacrificed flavor and nutrition.

Development of estuaries is particularly harmful. These are nurseries for many marine species.

Aquaculture is becoming more common as wild populations of seafood decline. The concentrated confinement causes pollution and displaces natural habitat.

The destruction of natural environments occurs around the world. These fields are in the Netherlands.

In the tropics coffee often accounts for the displacement of natural plant communities and the animals that depend on them. My annual coffee habit requires about 5 square meters of coffee plants.

The result of increasing development is a massive loss of native and plant and animal life. Several authors have referred to this as the sixth extinction, in comparison with mass extinctions that occurred in geologic history.

Some suggest that what we have referred to as the "wild" will no longer exist.

On top of all of these changes we are facing the reality associated with climate change. We must expect more droughts and floods, more record breaking hot and cold weather, more severe hurricanes and typhoons, rising sea level, and disruptions in biological communities.

This will decrease in agricultural productivity and increase the cost of food and other commodities.

Bill McKibben suggests the changes we have wrought have created a new world that significantly differs from the Earth we know. This is echoed by geologists who now recognize a new geologic epoch, the Anthropocene.

Simply knowing about the ecological problems often does not change behavior. I believe it is useful to put a face on extinction. I wish I could take all of you into a natural environment to witness the changes that are taking place. Let me try to give you a glimpse by showing some photos from a recent trip to Borneo.

Borneo is the third largest island in the world. It once held a very diverse array of animals and plants. However the diversity is rapidly being lost as the natural areas are being developed primarily for palm oil production.

We can see some pie charts on the right that shows the amount of deforestation. Less than 10% of the forest had been removed in 1950. In 2005 50% was gone. They estimated it would be 2/3 (~65%) gone by 2020. However, current data suggest it has already lost 75% of its forest.

Google Earth image of Borneo showing position of field station we worked at.

Flooding is common due to massive deforestation. The river loses about a meter a year due to erosion from flood water.

Earthworms maintain soil porosity. They reach over 50 cm in length and up to 2cm in diameter.

Wetlands are vital for amphibians.

Small sampling of frogs. Loss of this habitat would likely result in their extinction.

Look at that cute face. Who would want to see this species go extinct?

This one is common in the preserve, this bear was in a zoo in Kotakinabalu but we captured several images in the preserve with critter cams.

This was the first direct encounter with the endangered Sunda clouded leopard in the field station. We happened upon it about 4 AM on our way to conduct a bird census.

Many birds including hornbills.

Along the river it was common to see macaques in the trees. There are multiple species of primates including macaques are found in along the Kinabatanga River.

I did not get to see these but my students were working with a research group and they radio tracked and observed their behavior during our stay.

This endangered species is common in the preserve and it is a joy to watch their slow foraging. They depend on the various fruits of the forest and would not be able to survive in a palm oil plantation.

This species like the Bornean orangutan is only found in Borneo. It is endangered and will likely go extinct except for zoo collections, by 2050.

This is little critter is a Tarsier. It is a primate that eats insects and lives in the trees. This species cannot survive in oil palm or rubber plantations and has not been bred successfully in captivity. It will also likely go extinct if current trends continue.

I do not have time to share the multitude of fungi and plants that define the habitat and provide sustenance and shelter for all of the animal species. Some fungi glow in the dark.

This is a satellite view of the Kinabatanga River and Danau Girang. Note the encroachment of palm oil plantations. Deforestation has eliminated all but a few natural sites and these are not capable of supporting most of the species currently found in them.

The prime threat to the survival of these species is deforestation for palm oil. Here it is very close to the Kinebatanga River. They are allowed to plant less than 50 meters from the river. That is not enough to preserve any large animals and losing 1 m each year to erosion suggests the days of this ecosystem are numbered.

We passed many of these on our way back to Kotakinabalu.

This endangered species causes problems because they do not have enough room in the small reserves and cause damage when they move into oil palm plantations and other developed areas.

We read about 10 elephants that were poisoned on our way out of Malaysia. The baby was dependent on milk and thus did not die from eating poisoned food. It remains by its dead mother. This species will likely be extinct in the next half century.

Many food products contain palm oil. Buying palm oil drives deforestation. Look at the ingredients.

Most bath soaps also contain palm oil also known as palm kernelate. We tested the one on the right and it is one of the few that do not contain palm oil.

- First we must have a change of heart – we must care about others and the environment
- We must also realize that the transition we must make is a major one – a paradigm shift away from money and stuff to relationships and happiness
- Be assured that we can have a more fulfilling and "happier" life once we make the transition.

When we have truly embraced sustainability, the specifics actions will be revealed in each decision we make.

We must reconnect with the other parts of the system upon which we depend. We must think of others. Other people of the world, the plants and animals that share this space, and future generations whose fate will depend on the decisions we make.

In spite of some opinions population must be stabilized and ultimately reduced. The red is business as usual. Yellow is the UN's medium projections and green is the UN's low projection.

Just as important is reducing our individual ecological footprints. There are many ways of doing this. Lists help but the change of heart will allow one to see far more ways of reducing.

By reducing our numbers and collective footprint we can restore the balance of nature.

HEAD MASTER DAVE DELGADO

Mr. Delgado, a graduate of UC Berkeley, has 30 years of private school management experience including in various levels of administration, school development and organization, multi-campus accreditation, quality assurance, curriculum development, teacher selection and training, student assessment, student counseling, teaching, and problem-solving.

Environmental Conservation

I am passionate about wildlife preservation. I support many forms of conservation in several countries, I pitch in everything I can to these causes. But I don't call myself an environmentalist. On some level, each of us knows that this is the only earth we have, and that therefore our resources are finite, that means limited, this is all we got. However, you know, our day to day experiences, it's kind of easy to forget that we might have problems because we live in such a time of plenty. We seem to be able to get whatever we want, very easily, and uhhh there've been times in the past when we had scares of a shortage, a problem, and somehow, we managed to solve that particular problem. Whether it be fuel efficient vehicles, or some sort of clever way to solve it. So although human ingenuity and advancement of technology have solved some of these problems of scarcity that we thought unsolvable, I still think it would be foolish to think we can be rescued from wasteful practices inevitably. As an educator, I like playing around with words, I like working with definitions, I like to take words and narrow it down to definitions and try to make a concept easily understood with students. To that end, I see two components to the solution. I hear environmentalism a lot. When I isolate it, separate it out as that of a part of a political agenda, its political activism, its pressuring on leaders and hope the people who can make a difference for us, come up with a solution to able them with regulations that will help us. Large scale solutions involve very complex issues, but I will speak of the importance in a few minutes. Another word we've heard a lot is conservation. To give my definition of that, is a core virtue at the heart of this whole matter. It's what we can do as individuals right now without waiting for governments or somebody else to solve the problems for us. And what I like to define conservation is it's a concept of an ongoing effort, to get the full value out of every resource we can use. Course, we recycling is one of the well known ways to conserve, or to not waste our resources. It succeeds in its purpose for us to gain more value out of glass, or plastic, or metal, or lumber.

To continue the whole big picture, getting into your car, your gas powered car, driving to the collection center to hand in a few cans and get your 10 cents back, is not necessarily conserving. Recycling is usually thought of as taking bottles and cans to a collection center to be melted down, to be made into something else of additional value, but repurposing and reusing an item also allows it to go through a new life cycle. Recycling things, if you're able to repurpose them. So a simple way to think of repurposing: if you're reusing a water bottle, refilling a water bottle, you're getting more value out of that plastic, you haven't had to go purchase more plastic, you're getting more value out of not having to buy more. When you take the top off that bottle to use, to turn it into a cap for soup, you're giving it purpose and getting more value from that plastic. Then when you're out of ways to get more value, you can throw it in the garbage, or somehow get it to someone who can get you more value out of it. Try to get more value from that same resource. So if we're going to look at the big picture, only a recycling program of the right side is efficiency is actually serving the purpose of conserving resources. So back to repurposing: how can you measure the value of conservation when something is repurposed? Is there a way to know you're getting more value out of it? Repurposing and reusing resources is one of the most direct ways to conserve.

When I tore down this wall to make a larger space, I saved some of the lumber. Later I needed some stage platforms, which are of value to me, something that I did not have that I needed. Our art show used these large panels here for several years, until they were no longer nice looking enough to use for displaying art. So, I borrowed the garbage truck they had been loaned, and delivered them (the panels) to our school instead of the dump, where they were headed. That dozen 4x8 boards would've cost me $450 to purchase, the boards I saved from the previous wall would've cost me $150 too. So, a few hours of hammering, stapling, sweating, and couple bashed fingers, but new stage pieces are now ready for the stage band. So how can I measure this conservation? I'll discuss in more detail later, but in some circumstances, profit could be a good way to measure it, if you're doing the right thing. So I saved at least $500, what does that mean? Am I cheap? Do I want to save money? I just freed up $500 of financial resources that can be used to obtain a different value. That $500 also represents money as a placeholder for value, it represents every resource that could've gone into the lumber, you have to cut the tree, transport it, cut it into a board, drying it, transporting it to a store, the sales people selling it, you can see one act of conservation has many more effects. Following that recycled product, how many times it generates its own value, and the profit for the value, it's basically coming from nowhere, finding new use for this, and not using other resources.

So at this point, we realize, we have a pretty good general idea that recycling is a good way to conserve. So how do we make it happen more? It happens in education, it happens in stages.

Just casual observation, we've had beginnings of awareness, that will happen in this younger elementary school age, children told that recycling is a good thing to do. So what do they do? They remember to separate the garbage and they generally feel good about themselves because they did a good thing. We have the beginnings of action in highschool, here's an example: the student council starts a recycling program. It looks great on their college applications, but nobody remembers to supervise those cans, finally, they load the leaking bags into a friend's SUV, they take it to the collection station, and earn $10.13. But then they realize, it cost $25 to clean out their friend's vehicle, and now their data points say it wasn't worth it. They got $10, it cost $25. The program dies, student council forgets to tell everybody that recycling program ended, and the janitor is left with leaking, overfilled recycling containers at the start of summer break. But each step of this evolution is good, but the desire to do the action, to trying to organize some action. We have community, scientific backing, and sustainability at the college level. So here, the programs do get started. There's enough community participation to keep it going. Larger groups of people, but because there's research going on, they're getting credit for their research, now supported by scientific research, studies, and ongoing communication. Now, the available data points say the effort created more value than it cost.

To use Stanford as an example, they have a full recycling program already there. Their recycling program is large enough, they're a self-sustained community. The recycling program is large enough to show results, but not too large to study and to manage. And, the policies running it are set by educators, knowledgeable people, and then supported by the ongoing research and communication. There are questions I honestly wasn't too sure about for many years, and that's wondering 'Does recycling really conserve resources? Or does it use so many resources that it ends up being a wasteful thing?' Think of the trucks to pick up the recycling, the cost of the fuel, the person driving it (the truck). So many costs makes you wonder, are we actually conserving more or are we using more fossil fuels, and all things that might counteract that? I encourage anybody who's curious about that. What is shows is that all that still cost less than buying and processing new raw materials. In other words, there is still more value left in the item being recycled. We have a community now that developed a system to conserve, researched the effect, learned the value of the conservation value, and remain motivated to keep it up. There are many, many more that show that producing products recovered rather than raw materials uses significantly less energy, which results in less fossil fuels. I can't talk about conservation without answering the question, "What about our shared resources? Our air, our water?" Not only can we share the air we breathe, what's done is done by all of us. We just had a presentation show us the real consequences here. This is the point where the government enter the program.

Now we're back to environmentalism keeping pressure on world leaders and regulations and qualities of our shared resources. But regulations is a huge task that's not just closing down factories to clean the air pollution, or shutting down chemical plants to clean the water, the leaders want very smart and very educated people, like MIT smart, Harvard smart, really, really well educated experts and scientists to advise our leaders. They're going to need time, a lot of time to go into figuring out how to work together to keep our air and water clean. In the meantime, we can adopt and teach the virtue of conservation. From a young child using the recycling bins, to the fully developed university recycling system, with research and studies to support it, our voluntary and collective efforts to conserve will provide models and examples to offer insight to our leaders to pull things together. And I agree, conservation is vitally important to our future, we cannot expect our government to solve our problems from the top down unless they are met in the middle by our own individual support. Environmentalism and conservation are two separate ways to attack the problem.

JULIE BROCH

Julie Broch is an upcoming sophomore at Los Altos High School in California. She loves writing, sketching, and painting. She is also very interested in inventions helping to improve people's life style. As to the world's leading issues, she is particularly concerned with imminent environmental problems such as air pollution.

Fire and Air Pollution

We all know that air pollution is very harmful for human beings, but what are the causes? There are four main causes: the first being emissions from industrial plants and manufacturing activities. These emissions include smoke, sulfur dioxide and organic and particulate matter. Oftentimes these can be very harmful to human and animal health. Another cause is combustion from fossil fuels, which emit hazardous gases like oxides of nitrogen and Carbon Monoxide. Traffic is actually the leading cause of air pollution but factories and power plants also heavily damage our environment. The third cause is farming chemicals and household products. When these chemicals are released into the air they can cause serious health and respiratory issues. Lastly are the natural causes of air pollution, which includes forest fires, volcanic eruptions, and whirlwinds.

Today I would like to focus on one part of the natural causes of air pollution wildfires.

Wildfires are a prominent contributor to air pollution, especially in California where I currently reside.

For example, the Northern California Wildfires of October 2017. These fires claimed 245,000 acres of land and the lives of 44 people. It was a series of 250 wildfires that turned out to be one of the deadliest wildfire events in the past century in the US. 15 billion dollars in assets were lost and 89 buildings were destroyed. Around 10,000 firefighters fought the blaze and over 90,000 people were forced to evacuate their homes.

As a result of the fire, the air quality in Napa, a city where three major fires burned, reached a hazardous level on the Environmental Protection Agency scale and many residents fell sick from smoke inhalation. However, not only the people closest to the fires were affected. The winds carried the smoke and the air quality was unhealthy up to 100 miles away from where the fires actually took place. The toxic materials inside the walls of buildings were released into the air when burned. Upon inhalation, these toxic particles can go into lung tissues and the blood stream, causing heart and lung diseases. They can also cause adverse birth outcomes such as low birth weight, higher risk of illness and infection, and long term health problems. Children are the most sensitive to air pollution because their bodies are still developing.

There are several things people can do to reduce damages from the air pollution caused by fire. First, residents can leave the polluted area. Secondly, people should wear a mask when outdoors and also use air purification equipment in their homes. This wildfire event just goes to show how much damage fires can cause and how we must do our best to avoid them. People cause 85 percent of wildfires in the US, so in order to reduce the likeliness of wildfire occurrences, people need to be cautious of their actions outside and be aware of any potential fire hazards.

Hopefully, in the future, we can advance our technology so it can put out fires quickly before they cause any severe damage to both our land and our lungs.

DAVID ZHANG

David Zhang is going into his junior year at Mountain View High School in Mountain View, CA. He is really interested in physics and computer science, and loves to learn new things. He is also eager to find out how the world works and why it works like that. He hopes that he can use his skills to help change the world. He does robotics, volleyball, and computer programming but in his spare time, he likes to read, watch movies and talk with friends.

Tree Planting in Tibet

In places with high elevation, life is much harsher. High elevation mainly means a lack of oxygen, which is vital to sustaining our body. This makes it difficult for people to live and work there unless they have acclimated to it. Additionally, the climate at high altitudes is extremely cold and includes a large amount of rainfall and snowfall. This makes it much tougher to live in the area. Their lack of oxygen can also be attributed to the scarcity of plants in the area. However, a country like Ecuador is able to prosper in such conditions.

The reason is the presence of trees in the surrounding environment, which can supplement oxygen to the nearby inhabitants and reduce the effects of high altitude sickness. This leads to more people visiting and immigrating to the area, which grows the economy and helps the area develop.

Tibet is currently lacking in Trees compared to places like Ecuador, which contributes to its growing poverty. There have been efforts to plant trees in Qinghai, and many are working to increase the Oxygen in places like Yushu to help them grow. Higher places aren't supported at all. Tree planting is effective and helpful, as shown by the preliminary data I gathered. It has helped slightly increase the Oxygen content in Yushu and even in areas with higher elevation.

MICHELLE HUA

Michelle Hua is about to attend her sophomore year at Evergreen Valley High School. She loves reading, especially science fiction and fantasy. She also enjoys writing and drawing. Michelle Hua is currently the assistant editor of the lifestyle column for Rising Star Magazine.

Endangered Species in China

Hi, my name's Michelle Hua, and today I'll be talking about some endangered species in China.

The first species I'll be talking about is the South Chinese Tiger. They live in dense jungles and mountainous areas near Fujian, Hunan, and Guangdong. Male tigers weigh about 330 pounds and are about 8.5 feet long. The female tigers weigh about 242 pounds and are about 7.5 feet long. South Chinese tigers live for around 18 to 25 years. However, due to hunters and habitat loss, these tigers are critically endangered. In 2007, there were around 72 South Chinese tigers left, all in captivity. It is believed that these tigers are extinct in the wild. The current population of the South Chinese tigers is stable.

One of the more well-known endangered species is the giant panda. Pandas are found in bamboo forests near Sichuan, Shanxi, and Gansu. The males weigh 250 pounds, and the females weigh 220 lbs. On average, they are about 4 to six feet in length. Giant pandas live up to about 20 years. Their status is currently vulnerable, but their population is increasing. In 2014, there were about 1864 pandas found in the wild.

The third species I'll be discussing is the Asian Crested Ibis. These birds live in forests and wetlands near Shaanxi. They used to be found in multiple countries in Asia, but now only live in forests and wetlands near Shaanxi. Asian Crested Ibises weigh 2.2 lbs on average and are about 1.8 feet long. These birds live for about 16 years. Asain Crested Ibises have made a dramatic comeback. In the 1980s, there were only about 10 left, but now, there are about 330 in total. Their population is currently increasing.

The last species I'll be discussing is the Chinese alligator. Chinese alligators live in wetlands near Anhui. They weigh about 79.4 pounds and are about 6.6 feet long. These reptiles live for about 18 to 25 years. They are critically endangered, with only about 120 left in the wild. Chinese alligators are one of the most endangered crocodiles in the entire world. Though there are very few of these alligators left, their population is currently stable.

There are over 1400 endangered species in China. The best way that we can help to save them is to spread awareness and to donate to organizations that are helping to preserve them. The more that people know about these endangered species, the easier it will be to save them from extinction.

ERICK MOISES XU LI

Erick was born in Sinaloa, which is a state in the north of Mexico. He studies at Eton School in Mexico City and he's going to 12th grade. He is very interested in science and technology, especially AI and Robotics. He wants to be a robotics engineer in the future. Erick wants to study applied mathematics at college.

The Use of Robotics to Improve Environmental Conditions

The effects of climate change become more dramatic every year. As humans, we are experiencing changes in temperature and extreme natural disasters are sweeping across the world. Plants and animals are also affected by the changing climate, with delicate species at risk and crops dying in extreme heat and drought.

Globally, robot developers and researchers are using their passion for robotics to help the environment. One robot won't solve all of our problems, but together we can all work to make a difference. Here are 15 ways robots are fighting climate change.

Climate change startups tend to pick a specific element of environmental harm and solve a problem for it. For CEO of SkyGrow, it's planting trees. He developed his company to plant more trees than we are cutting down — and not just in remote forests like the Amazon. The team at SkyGrow developed the Growbot, an unmanned vehicle that plants trees 10 times faster than a human can, at about half the cost.

Growbot plants established trees instead of seeds, because established trees have a greater chance of succeeding in their new location. Stewart and his team plan to manufacture 4,500 Growbots, helping forests recover everywhere.

Researchers are working to recreate the behavior and functions of plants to study the natural environment.

They have realized the best way to study the environment is to use the same methods plants use to filter air, water, and other chemicals that they're exposed to. The robot plant they have developed even has a mini 3D printer that helps the roots "grow," allowing researchers to explore the soil that plants are exposed to.

In Australia recently covered the development of a "Row-bot" developed by the University of Bristol that digests pollution in the water and turns it into energy. The robot swims around, ingesting microbes which then power the boat's motor. It's really no different than a whale shark filter feeding krill and using that food energy to travel around the ocean.

According to Jonathan Rossiter, who hosted a TED talk about these robots, this technology could help reduce the impact of tankers that flush their oil tanks into the sea and of chemicals that are washed into rivers and wind up in the oceans.

BRIAN (RUIBO) WU

Brian Wu is a sophomore student at Waterford School. He developed interests in nature science since he was young, especially in math, engineering, and artificial intelligence. He also has strong curiosity and manipulative ability. He has participated in model aircraft competitions since primary school. In addition, he also loves traditional Chinese calligraphy, and has won gold in the national calligraphy competitions many times.

Thermal Pollution

We all know that smog and pollution is bad for our health: but exactly how bad is it? Smog is a kind of air pollutant. The word "smog" combines both the words smoke and fog, originally created to describe the smoky fog in London in the 19th century. Researchers soon discovered that smog was composed of nitrogen oxides, sulfur oxides, ozone, smoke, and other particulates. Our human-made smog is derived from coal, vehicular, and industrial emissions, forest and agricultural fires, and photochemical reactions of these emissions.

But why does this all matter? About 5.5 million people die prematurely each year proving smog is indeed a serious problem in many cities and continues to harm human health. All the different particulates are especially harmful to senior citizens, children, and people with heart and lung conditions. It cause shortness of breath, wheezing, and coughing, additionally, causing eye and nose irritation and dries out the protective membranes of the nose and throat. While these symptoms may just seem annoying, long term effects also come into play. Smog inflames breathing passages and decrease the lungs' working capacity, resulting in children's development of asthma, and interferes with the body's ability to fight infection, thus increasing children's dispositions to other diseases. The effects of inhaling particulate matter additionally include asthma, lung cancer, respiratory diseases, cardiovascular disease, premature delivery, birth defects, low birth weight, and premature death. In fact, hospitals oftentimes notice an increase in patients during periods when ozone levels are high.

But there is still light at the end of the tunnel. There are many ways to decrease our emissions, for example, driving less. Now although this may seem unfeasible at first, there are always alternatives such as carpooling. However if this is not possible,we can at least begin by getting regular tune ups for cars. We can fuel up our houses during the cooler hours of the day, whether that be simply turning on the sprinklers at nighttime. Emissions may also be reduced if we don't use products with VOCs or volatile organic compounds which can easily turn into gases. Additionally, driving and manufacturing electric cars will heavily reduce the air pollution that is rampant in our society. And of course, there are many many more simple things we can do.

The impact is clear. We only have one planet and by polluting it so heavily, we risk the safety and wellbeing of our future generations. Yet at what the end of the day we stand together. Mother Nature has given so much to us: it's time we help her back.

KEVIN YOU

My name is Kevin You. I have just graduated 10th grade from Palo Alto High School. I have lived in China for 7 years and the US for 9 years. In China, I lived in Zhejiang province, Hangzhou city. In the US, I lived in the bay area in California. I like to play soccer, chess, and cycling.

Ecological Effects of Dams

Dams are barriers that restricts the flow of water in rivers. The reservoirs created are obviously useful for irrigation, industrial use, or human consumption. Furthermore, dams are often used to generate hydroelectric power, which supplies over 60% of renewable energy. However, dams are not perfect, and can create harmful environmental impacts. Today, we shall examine a particular river along with the dams on it and see its environmental impacts. This river is the Mekong river, 2600 miles long and passes through China and much of Southeast Asia. There exist 11 major dams along that river. Also, there are more than 500 known species of fish inhabiting the river.

Now, dams do not directly pollute the water or the air, but it can have large environmental impacts through changing the environment and affecting natural habitats in the dam area. One impact is that the flow rate of water becomes unpredictable. During the dry seasons, water levels tend to be exceptionally high, while in the wet seasons, the water levels are very low, in northern Thailand.

Another quite large impact of the damns is sedimentation and erosion. Most sediments that flow in the river, and they tend to be stopped by the dam. Thus, in the downstream region, sediments from the riverbed are pushed away, but not being replaced by the sediments upstream.

Next, dams also affect the fish living in the river. Dams literally block fish from their migratory paths. This particularly affects migratory fish such as salmon to reach their spawning grounds. Also, a reservoir can change the water temperature, which in turn may affect native fish and plants in the river and on land. Finally, dams can block nutrients from reaching downstream, hence reducing biodiversity downstream. Currently, dams on the Mekong river traps much of the nutrients that fertilizes delta fields ad feed fish throughout the system, which deprives downstream ecosystems. In addition, the fishing business and aquaculture has been impacted due to fewer fish and marine life.

Luckily, there are solutions to these issues. Specifically, regarding migratory fish, fish ladders has been increasingly popular in helping fish reach their spawning grounds upstream. A fish ladder allows fish to pass through the dam by swimming and leaping up a series of relatively low steps. Fish ladders have a mixed record in effectiveness for different rivers and types of fish. Next, to deal with nutrition/sedimentation blockade, small holes can be created near the bottom of dams to allow nutrients on the riverbed to pass through. Similarly, side streams or spillways can be constructed to maintain a constant water flow rate and counteract flooding. At last, students need to be educated on the downsides of building and operating dams.

ALEX BAO

Alex Bao is about to attend his sophomore year in the Shanghai School international division. He loves literature, especially in both macro and micro economics. He'd like to be involved in specific field research. He is eager to understand history under the context of people, economy, and technologies, how the combination of these factors formed the world in which we live today. In his spare time, he likes to watch movies, play basketball, and participate in swimming competitions.

Plastic in the Ocean

Plastic, the wonder material that we use for everything and which pollutes our environment, is perhaps the most harmful of trash, because it does not readily break down in nature. We've probably all have been to the ocean and we know the beautiful of it. We might also seen videos like a sea turtle with a straw stick in its nose, or a whale that have eaten tons of plastic in its stomach. Some of these incidents have hopping endings, but of them in reality do not.

Approximately 8 million tons of plastic goes into the ocean every year. Plastic bags or straws and plastic waste will go into the stomach of these sea species. Plastic is toxic, These toxins have also been found in many fish in the ocean.When animal inject plastics, it also cause life threatening problems to them.

If we don't do something now, we could be facing hundred million metric tons in the ocean in less than 10 years. One of the reasons that plastic pollution is such a problem is that plastic will not easily go away, it will stay for hundred years. Instead, plastic breaks down into ever-smaller particles

Our goal is to cut down the amount of plastic entering the ocean by half within a decade.

We believe that the long term solution to plastic in our oceans is to teach more people about the harmful effect that plastic carry.

1. Carry a reusable water bottle. Not only does a refillable bottle make good environmental sense, it's good for your bank account. Three cheers for staying hydrated without contributing to plastic pollution in the ocean!
2. Go straw-free. Every day, Americans use 500 million straws, which aren't recyclable and often end up in oceans. Next time you're eating out at your favorite restaurant, just tell them you don't need a straw!
3. Recycle Properly. This should go without saying, but when you use single-use (and other) plastics that can be recycled, always be sure to recycle them.
4. Support Bans Many municipalities around the world have enacted bans on single use plastic bags, takeout containers, and bottles. You can support the adoption of such policies in your community.
5. Pick up litter. The important thing is that we all do something, no matter how small.

This is bigger than all of us individually, even people like you can help to solve it

KEVIN ZHANG

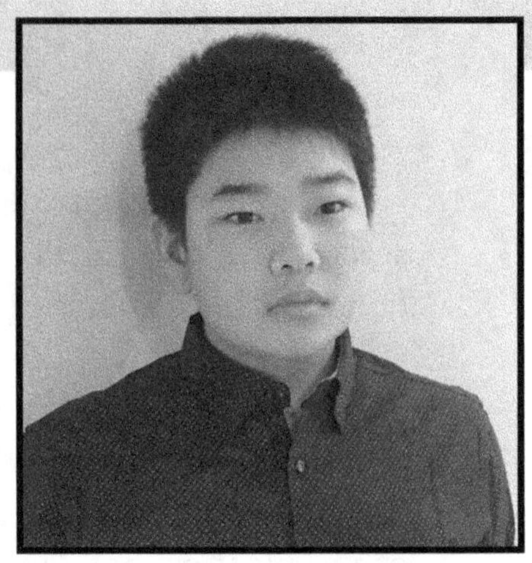

Kevin Zhang is a rising 9th grader about to attend Mountain View High School in Mountain View, California. He enjoys video games, science, math, and learning new things.

Air Pollution

Air pollution is harmful substances in the air. It can refer to chemicals from factories, car emissions, dust, pollen, soot, ozone, etc. It is split into two categories: indoor and outdoor.

Particulate matter is any harmful materials in the air. The particulate matter scale is used to measure the size of those materials. Particles less than 2.5 microns in diameter, or PM2.5, can easily get into the lower respiratory system of the human body and cause damage. The Air Quality Index is used by governments around the world to measure the amount of pollution in the air and to communicate to the public how safe it is to be active outside.

Air Pollution is related to around 6 million deaths per year, 1 million of which are Chinese. Coarse particles can reach the upper respiratory system and finer particles can reach even deeper. Particles can cause respiratory problems, eye and nose irritation, heart disease, cognitive impairment, and possibly Alzheimer's disease. Exposed exposure can also cause birth defects and cancer.

Polluted air can cause many forms of damage to the surrounding environment. Eutrophication, or excessive amounts of nutrients in natural bodies of water, can be caused by polluted runoff or rain. Dense plant growth can then occur and block out sunlight and take nutrients meant for animal life. Acid rain, or rain mixed with chemicals, can destroy habitats and crops. Air pollution can wear away against the ozone layer, which protects the earth from ultraviolet light. Climate change can occur from gas trapped beneath the atmosphere of the earth.

However, you can still help with this issue. Reducing car trips, and instead walking, biking, or using public transportation will reduce the car emissions you contribute to. Getting smog checks and maintaining car engines will make sure your car won't be excessively emitting. Tires can sometimes contain gases harmful to the environment. Fixing leaking tires will prevent the tires from releasing harmful gases into the environment. Reducing the use of wood stoves and fireplaces will reduce the amount of gas and smoke that goes into the air. Make sure to save energy whenever possible and buy energy-efficient products. Quitting smoking or restraining yourself from smoking indoors or where smoking is prohibited will greatly benefit public and indoor air quality.

CHRISTINA HUA

Christina Hua is an upcoming senior at Evergreen Valley High School. She likes music since she plays in her school's Symphonic Band. She loves animals and wants to help keep animals safe.

Animal Protection

Animal abuse is something that often sparks debates, as some people want them to have rights, while others take advantage of the fact that they don't have a voice. However, animals help us in day to day life, and since we use animals for food and labor, I believe that we should at least treat them with kindness.

There are two types of animal cruelty: neglect and intentional cruelty. Neglect constitutes of not providing animals with basic needs by a forgetful owner, puppy farming, and hoarding. This may cause your pet to be removed from the household. The cause of neglectful ownership may be unintentional, or it could be something more severe, such as trauma as a child or elder that reflects onto the animal. For example, the trope of a crazy cat lady could actually be a hoarding problem. When someone begins to hoard pets, their ability to take care of all of them diminishes, which can result in death for the animal.

Intentional Cruelty means that the abuser is purposely causing harm towards an animal, such as maiming and torture. Dogfighting and physical harm or abuse are some of the more well known examples of intentional cruelty. This may be because of severe discipline, where the owner physically harms the animal to make it behave, or domestic violence. Though there isn't a set solution to animal abuse, what we can do at the moment is to advocate for better treatment of animals or at least informing the abuser about their actions.

STANLEY LUO

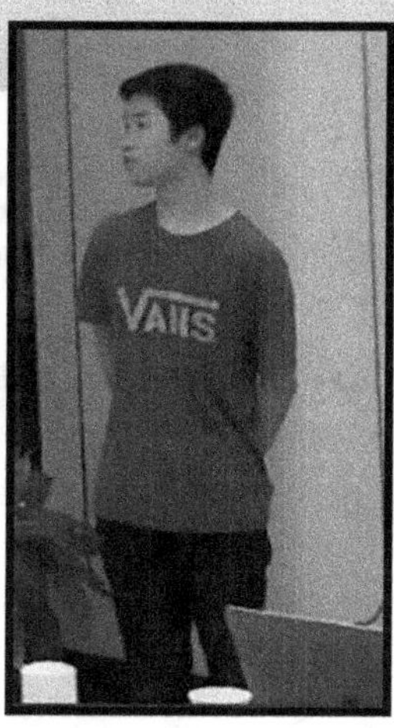

My name is Stanley Luo, also known in Chinese as Luo Cen Ling. I am 15 years old and was born in China. I am currently studying in New Jersey, at a high school. I am more of an introverted person because I'm shy. But if you get to know me, you will learn that my favorite hobbies are wrestling, sleeping and eating.

MICHAEL CHANG

Michael is a rising senior at Homestead High School in Cupertino. His main hobbies include cinematography, traveling, scale modeling, studying aviation, and watching movies.

An Agent of Change

So there have been so many amazing presentations warning us about the dangers of climate change, but have we ever considered what we can do to stop this change? Climate change is a universal problem, so here I am going to show you one of the many ways to do your part.

One of the easiest ways is to partner with a volunteer organization that you believe in. In my case, I chose Agents of Change, a nonprofit started by my local Congressman Ro Khanna of California's 17th Congressional District. I mainly chose this organization since as the incumbent Congressman of my district, he has the ability to get things done quick, giving our organization an expedited advantage in making our mark on our community.

We have to first identified the problem that plagues our environment. We decided that we should be responsible for the environment not only in the traditional sense of nature and conservationism, but also the urban or suburban environments and communities we grow up in. Being from the San Francisco Bay Area, where homelessness is an extremely visible and growing problem, we wanted to focus on their lack of hygiene.

In order to make people want to save nature, we expected that they needed to experience it first, so we focused on helping organizations near cities that would benefit from more visits. We also wanted to direct our efforts towards elementary school kids, the future of our generation. Since it is rather dangerous to approach homeless people on the street, the only effective way was to partner with other relief organizations and provide supplies or volunteer work with them.

Our first project was elementary advocacy, where we brought elementary school children to after-school learning and activity sessions, leading them in a range of activities such as planting gardens, teaching them to appreciate nature, and warning them of global climate change.

The organizations that we partnered with were also nature-related. Our City Forest, a small plantation for native Californian trees, got help from our organization to help expand its operations and bring back the fight against invasive species. Animal Assisted Happiness was a special organization as well. Their mission, to bring farm animals and birds to autistic or terminally ill communities, was especially important, giving parents a glimpse into the positive effects nature has on our community.

So what are the numbers, the impact of this mission? With our help, Animal Assisted Happiness, in the last year we've partnered with them to provide volunteer work and other forms of assistance, has logged 30,000 volunteer hours and has been able to make over 2300 visits to disabled children.

Last but not least, our final project, codenamed Care for Comfort, partnered with the Silicon Valley Sacred Heart Community Service to run fundraisers and donations to pack for homeless distribution, of which includes Hygiene Products, Clothing, Everyday Supplies in order to make them more approachable by others, hopefully cascading into better sense of community for all.

www.ingramcontent.com/pod-product-compliance
Lightning Source LLC
Chambersburg PA
CBHW080351030726
47598CB00009B/2704